Meet the Horses

Appaloosa Horses

by Rachel Grack

Bullfrog Books, an imprint of Jump! Library by FlutterBee

Bullfrog Books

Ideas for Parents and Teachers

Bullfrog Books let children practice reading informational text at the earliest reading levels. Repetition, familiar words, and photo labels support early readers.

Before Reading

- Discuss the cover photo. What does it tell them?
- Look at the picture glossary together. Read and discuss the words.

During Reading

- "Walk" through the book with the reader. Discuss new or unfamiliar words. Sound them out together.
- Look at the photos together. Point out the photo labels.

After Reading

- Prompt the child to think more. Ask: Have you ever seen an Appaloosa horse? What color were its spots?

Bullfrog Books are published by Jump!
3500 American Blvd W, Suite 150
Bloomington, MN 55431
www.jumplibrary.com

Jump! is a division of FlutterBee Education Group.

Library of Congress Cataloging-in-Publication Data

Names: Koestler-Grack, Rachel A., 1973– author
Title: Appaloosa horses / by Rachel Grack.
Description: Bloomington, MN: Jump!, Inc., [2026]
Series: Meet the horses | Includes index.
Audience: Ages 5–8
Identifiers: LCCN 2025011468 (print)
LCCN 2025011469 (ebook)
ISBN 9798896622321 (hardcover)
ISBN 9798896622338 (paperback)
ISBN 9798896622345 (ebook)
Subjects: LCSH: Appaloosa horse—Juvenile literature
Classification: LCC SF293.A7 .K64 2026 (print)
LCC SF293.A7 (ebook)
DDC 636.1/3—dc23/eng/20250716
LC record available at https://lccn.loc.gov/2025011468
LC ebook record available at https://lccn.loc.gov/2025011469

Editor: Katie Chanez
Designer: Molly Ballanger
Content Consultant: Becky Robb Hotzler; Wells Creek Wild Mustang Sanctuary; This Old Horse, Inc.

Photo Credits: Rita_Kochmarjova/Shutterstock, cover; Olga_i/Shutterstock, 1, 9, 23bm; Eric Isselee/Shutterstock, 3, 22, 24; catnap72/iStock, 4; Lenkadan/Shutterstock, 5, 14–15 (left); Photos by By Deb Alperin/Getty, 6–7, 23tm; Zuzana Tillerova/Adobe Stock, 8, 23tl, 23bl; Shawn Hamilton CLiX/Adobe Stock, 10–11, 23br; rdonar/Shutterstock, 12–13, 23tr; Marie Charouzova/Shutterstock, 14–15 (right); Kobby Dagan/Dreamstime, 16; Margo Harrison/Shutterstock, 17; ID-VIDEO/Shutterstock, 18–19; Julia Shepeleva/Adobe Stock, 20–21.

Printed in the United States of America at Corporate Graphics in North Mankato, Minnesota.

Table of Contents

Spotted Horses

Horses run!

They have spots.

They are Appaloosa horses.

Their **coats** are different.

No two are the same.

Cocoa is a **bay**.
His **mane** is short.

Sugar has spots on her **muzzle**.

Leo has white **stockings**.

stocking

stripe

Look at this **hoof**.

It has stripes.

Neat!

Their eyes have white.

Other horses do not.

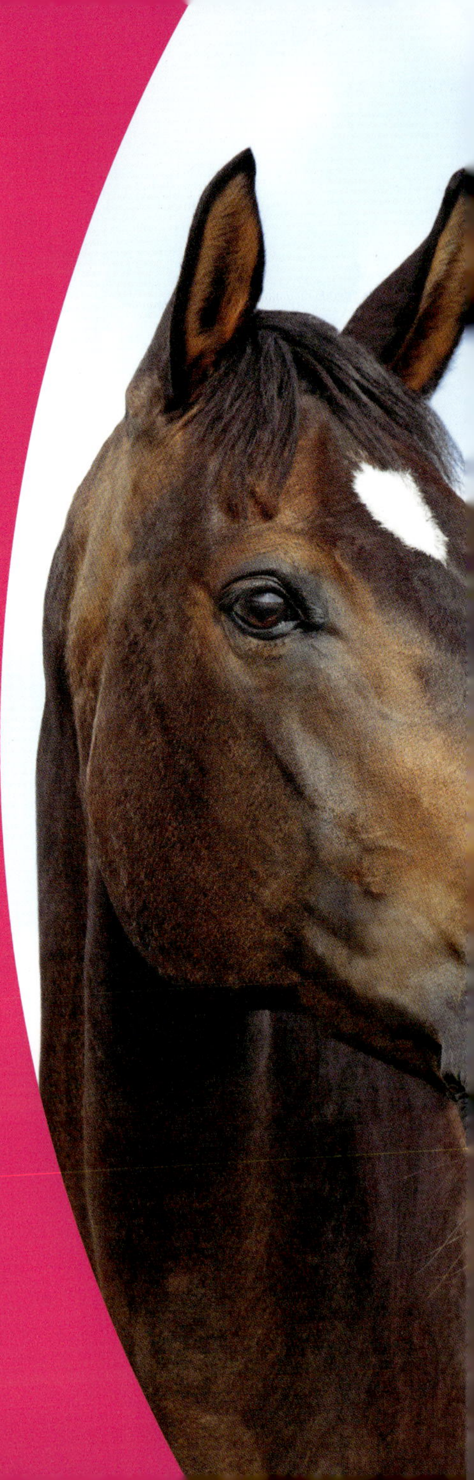

white

Bella runs around a barrel.

She is fast.

Outlaw runs after a cow.

He works hard.

Mack gives rides.

Fun!

Spirit is a friend.

Good boy!

A Look at an Appaloosa Horse

What are the parts of an Appaloosa horse? Take a look!

Picture Glossary

bay
A horse with a brown or red-brown coat and a black mane and tail.

coats
Hair on horses.

hoof
The hard part that covers a horse's foot.

mane
The hair on a horse's head and neck.

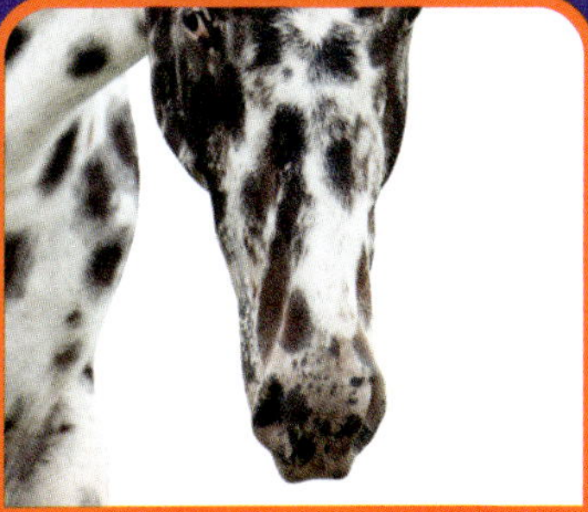

muzzle
An animal's nose and mouth.

stockings
The white markings on a horse's lower legs that look like stockings, or socks.

Index

To Learn More

FACT SURFER

Finding more information is as easy as 1, 2, 3.

1. Go to **www.factsurfer.com**
2. Enter "**Appaloosa horses**" into the search box.
3. Choose your book to see a list of websites.